Bringing Together

MAXINE KUMIN

Bringing Together

UNCOLLECTED EARLY POEMS

1958–1988

W. W. NORTON & COMPANY

NEW YORK   LONDON

The poems in this book, sometimes in slightly different form, have been gleaned from the following collections: *Halfway*; *The Privilege*; *The Nightmare Factory*; *Up Country*; *House, Bridge, Fountain, Gate*; *The Retrieval System*; *The Long Approach*; *Our Ground Time Here Will Be Brief*; and *Nurture*.

Copyright © 2003 by Maxine Kumin

Manufacturing by The Courier Companies, Inc.
Book design by Chris Welch
Production manager: Anna Oler

LIBRARY OF CONGRESS CATALOGING-IN-PUBLICATION DATA
Kumin, Maxine, date.
Bringing together : uncollected early poems, 1958–1988 / by Maxine Kumin.—1st ed.
p. cm.
ISBN 0-393-05766-6 (hardcover)
I. Title.
PS3521.U638B75 2003
811'.54—dc21

2002156436

W. W. Norton & Company, Inc., 500 Fifth Avenue, New York, N.Y. 10110
www.wwnorton.com

W. W. Norton & Company Ltd., Castle House, 75/76 Wells Street London
W1T 3QT

1 2 3 4 5 6 7 8 9 0

To Janeo, firstborn

CONTENTS

I

II

III

IV

I

A MORTAL DAY OF NO SURPRISES

This morning a frog in the bathtub
and not unhappy with his lot
hunkering over the downspout
out there in the pasture.
Strawberries, morever,
but not the bearing kind, scrub
growth, many-footed pretenders,
running amok in the squash hills and valleys.

Out of here! I say
ripping the lime-green tendrils from
their pinchhold on my zucchini blossoms
and out! with a thrust of the grain scoop
to the teal-blue frog who must have fallen
from the sky in a sneakstorm that slipped
in between 2 and 3 A.M. when
even God allows for a nap.

Last night at that sneakstorm time
(God sleeping, me working out
among the rerun dreams)
two white-throated sparrows
woke me to make their departmental claims—
Old Sam Peabody peabody pea—
wrangling like clerks in adjoining bureaus
only to recommence at dawn
saying their names and territories.

Now for good measure
the dog brings home one-half a rank
woodchuck no angel spoke up for
but won't say where he's banked
the rest of the treasure
and one of this year's piglets
gets loose again by rooting under,
emerging from mud like a crawfish
to stumble across the geese's path
and have an eye pecked bloody by the gander.

All this in a summer day
to be gone like cloth at the knees
when the dark comes down
ancient and absolute as thistles.

A day predictable as white-throat whistle.
A day that's indistinguishable
from thirty others, except the mare's
in heat and miserable,
flagging, rubbing her tail bare.

When I'm scooped out of here
all things animal
and unsurprised will carry on.
Frogs still will fall into those
stained old tubs we fill
with trickles from the garden hose.
Another blue-green prince will sit
like a friend of the family
guarding the doomspout.
Him asquat at the drainhole,
me gone to crumbs in the ground
and someone else's mare to call
to the distant stallion.

STRUT

Every morning to guard against glut I chop
zucchini zealots for the lambs
who are not particularly grateful.
They prefer mashed apples and fresh grain.

Every morning I rethink how common green
—pond scum, a thousand sumac sprouts
orchard and rye grass, birdsfoot trefoil
milkweed, poke, dock, dill, sorrel

bush and shrub, soft and hard woods, all
leafy-headed—must go down again in
frost and come again. Is this a deep
head-tilting meditative thought, or

vernal instinctual, nothing more?
Here come the marbleized rat-wet new foals
blowing blue bubbles like divers into air
on their feet in minutes finding

the mares' teats by trial-and-error blind
butting stagger-dance. And here comes
cakewalk-cocky with the whole mess
of birth and rebirth the strut of the season.

Almost bliss.

IN THE UPPER PASTURE

In the evergreen grove that abuts the pasture we are
limbing low branches, carting away deadwood,
cutting close to the trunk so the sap does not bleed,
to make a shelter, a run-in for foals and their mares.
We will not shorten the lives of these hemlocks and pines
in the afternoon of our own lives, yet I am sad
to think that the dell will outlast us and our bloodlines.

Is this a pastoral? Be not deceived
by the bellows of leathery teats giving suck,
by the fringe of delicate beard that pricks
its braille notes on the muzzle of the newborn.
When instinct whinnies between dam and foal
at night in the rain, do not be lulled.
Each of us whimpers his way through the forest alone.

With galvanized nails and scrap lumber we fence off
a triad of trees that have grown so close to each other
a young horse darting through might be taken prisoner.
Let the babies be safe here, let them lie down on pine duff
away from the merciless blackflies, out of the weather.
Under the latticework of old trees, let me stand
pitchstreaked and pleasured by this small thing we have done.

TONIGHT

Tonight the peepers are as loud as all
the grandmothers of the world's canaries, those
Petey- and Dicky-birds trilling vibratos
from their baggage-handle perches, perpetual
singing machines stoned on seeds of hemp.

Tonight the peepers are a summer camp-
ful of ten-year-olds still shrilling after taps.
Winter will have us back with cold so harsh
our nose hairs freeze. Martens will spring the traps.
But peepers tonight—spring peepers hallow the marsh.

FIVE SMALL DEATHS IN MAY

Somehow a mole has swum too far
downstream from the tunnel and drowned
in the pond. On his nose the star
he wears for a wise fifth hand
is losing its pink. His eyepits blacken.
Now the sun can sink
into those two particulars
and eat away the last wires.

A milk snake has come to this cup
of straw at the cleft of a rock.
It has drunk the good yolk up.
When the meadowlark flicks back
she turns and turns like a dog
making a place to lie down.
The shell specks fly out between her legs.
They are flecked lavender and brown.

A heron is fishing for minnows.
In the shadow of the bird
they crowd together
lying straight out to leeward
a see-through army in the shallows

as still as grains in a rice bowl.
Scooped up they go down whole
exchanging one wet place for another.

The owl, old monkey face
will have his nightly mouse
culled from the tribe
disgorging here and there
down in his pine-lined bog
and on the pathway to the house
a chip of rib, a flake of leg
a tuft of hair.

I will not sing the death of Dog
who lived a fool to please his King.
I will put him under the milkweed bloom
where in July the monarchs come
as spotted as he, as rampant, as enduring.

THE GRACE OF GELDINGS IN RIPE PASTURES

Glutted, half-asleep, browsing in
timothy grown so tall I see them
as through a pale-green stage scrim

they circle, nose to rump,
a trio of trained elephants.
It begins to rain, as promised.

Bit by bit they soak up drops
like laundry dampened to be ironed.
Runnels adorn them. Their sides

drip like the ribs of very broad
umbrellas. And still they graze
and grazing, one by one let down

their immense, indolent penises
to drench the everlasting grass
with the rich nitrogen

that repeats them.

Philosophers penned up all day
on polders rescued from the bay,
they feast on a glut of grass.

By noon they've reached fulfill-
ment, raise their heads
and discourse on free will.
or ruminate upon the clouds, the *zees.*

Their eyes are like those pictures that enclose
a comely lady looking in
a pier glass that reflects
a comely lady looking in a glass.

Rembrandt knew these animal eyes
globed as green figs, and Van Eyck caught
inside their opaque irises fields of thought,
deep vistas of surmise

where cows reflect themselves, reflect and chew,
while of their number some
think simply as I do
O to be that full, that full and dumb.

A NEW ENGLAND GARDENER GETS PERSONAL

Kale
curls. Laughs at cold rain.
Survives leaf-snapping hail.
Under snow, stays green.
Comes crisp as a handclap
to the bowl
then lies meekly down
with lettuces and cole.

Willy-nilly
after years of no peppers
a glut of them
perfect as Peter Piper's.
Only piccalilli
will get shut of them.
None grow riper
none redden in this clime
but such sublime
pectorals! Such green hips!
No Greek torso comes
more nobly equipped.

What ails you, cherry tomato?
Why do you blossom and fail to bear?
Is it acid rain you're prey to
or nicotine in the air?

Are you determinate or not,
wanting trellises,
strings to cling to from the pot?
What evil spell is this?

Apple on a stalk, kohlrabi
grows fronds in its ears.
Stands stiff as a bobby
when the Queen appears.
Quoth she, *my dears*
eat this pale knob when small
or not at all.

Carrot wants company in bed.
Presses
to be held on either side
by purslane, chickweed
and coarser grasses.
Once these are pulled, puts down alone
its secret orange cone.

The dreaded rutabaga comes,
a dull gargantuan.
Winters, like money in the bank
this bulbous swede
is eaten by cattle and people in need.

THE FOOD CHAIN

The Hatchery's old bachelor, Henry Manley
backs his pickup axle-deep into my pond
opens the double tub of brookies
and begins dipping out his fingerlings.
Going in, they glint like chips of mica.

Henry waits a while to see them school up.
They flutter into clumps like living rice grains.
He leaves me with some foul-smelling pellets
and instructions how to sow them on the water
a few days until they smarten and spread out.

What *he* does is shoot kingfishers with his air rifle.
They ate two thousand fry on him last weekend.
Herons? They hunt frogs, but watch for martens.
They can clean a pond out overnight.
He stands there busy with his wrists and looking savage.

Knowing he knows we'll hook his brookies
once they're a sporting size, I try for something
but all the words stay netted in my mouth.
Henry waves, guns the engine. His wheels spin
then catch.

NIGHT, THE PADDOCK, SOME DREAMS

All the loud night cocooned
in my farmhouse bed I hear
stones knock, an owl begin
and the snuffles of my mare

who sleeps in fits and starts
warily upright
under the buckshot stars.
Only with the first light

she goes ungainly down
folding her leg sticks in
to lie like some overgrown
dachshund-turned-dinosaur

her neck important as
Victorian furniture
her backbone ridged and strong
as the Seven Hills of Rome.

The ear, according to
postmodernist Hassan
has no eyelids. True.
Sight merges, one with sound

for grazers who crop in dreams
clover and timothy
wound up in vetch, such greens
as the acreage allows.

I dream instead gaunt cows
heads down in their own dung
and crueler images:
the ribs of all my dears

picked famine-dry and hung
for lesser foragers.
Far worse than dreams go on.
Leave people out of this.

Let the loud night be gone
and let the old mare rouse
from dampness in her bones
and safely browse.

COUNTRY HOUSE

After a long presence of people,
after the emptying out,
the laying bare,
the walls break into conversation.
Their little hairlines ripple
and an old smile
crosses the chimney's face.

The same flies
drawn to the windowpanes
buzz endlessly from thirst.
Field mice coast down
a forgotten can of bacon fat.
Two clocks tick themselves witless.
October, clutching its blankets,
sidles from room to room
where the exhausted doors
now speak to their stops,
four scrubbed stones of common quartz.

They are gone,
those hearty moderns who came in
with their plastic cups and spoons
and restorative kits

for stripping the woodwork,
torn between making over
and making do.
At their leavetaking
the thin beds exhale.
The toilet bowl blinks,
its eye full of antifreeze.

As after a great drought
the earth opens its holes
to raise the water table,
the stairs undo their buttons.
The risers, each an individual,
slip out of plumb.
Seams, pores and crazings unpucker
making ready for frost.
A tongue of water
circles the cellar wall
and locks itself in.

Soon the raccoon will come
with his four wise hands
to pick the carcass
and the salt-worshiping porcupine

will chew sweat from the porch swing.
Red squirrels will invade the attic,
mice housekeep between floors.
Caught and fastened, this house
will lean into the January blizzard
letting its breath go sour,
its rib cage stiffen.

NOTES ON A BLIZZARD

Snow makes Monday as white
at supper as breakfast was.
All day I watch for our wild
turkeys, the ones you've tamed
with horse corn, but only the old
gobbler comes, toeing out on his henna feet.
Small-headed, pot-bellied, he stands
too tall—I need to think this—
to tempt a raccoon. Tonight, not
turning once, I sleep in your empty space
as simply as a child in a child's cot.

Tuesday, the sky still spits
its fancywork. Wherever
the chickadees swim to is secret.
The house breathes, you occur to me as
that cough in the chimney, that phlegm-fall
while the wood fire steams, hard put
to keep itself from going out.

Wednesday, the phone's dead.
The dog coils his clay tail across
his eyes and runs, closing in
on a rabbit. Late afternoon,

in a lull, I go out on snowshoes
to look the woods over.
Above the brook a deer
is tearing bark from a birch tree,
as hungry as that, tearing
it off in strips the way
you might string celery.

Only liars keep diaries.
I didn't see him curling his lip
or the papery festoons pulled free.
Only his backside humping away
clumsily through the deep snow.
Only the half-moon hoofprints refilling
and the cupful of raisin droppings.

Thursday, the wind turns. We're down
to snow squalls now. Last night you walked
barefoot into my dream. The mice
wrangling on all sides
raised thunder in my head
nothing but lath and plaster
between them and the weather.

It's Friday. The phone works.
You're driving north. Your voice
is faint, as if borne across
clothesline and tin cans from the treehouse.
The turkeys show up again
flopping under the kitchen window
like novice swimmers daring the deep end.
Low on corn, I offer jelly beans.
The sun comes out eventually,
a bedded woman, one
almond eye open.

II

THE PARIS POEM

August, 1944

Eighteen and barefoot in Manhattan
on the morning of the False Liberation
with *le jour de gloire,* that fatuous call
to love and honor blatting in my head
I drank a split of New York State champagne
and chewed on garlic bread
with my displaced Parisian, Jean-Paul.

And then Fifth Avenue fell under us
uptown and downtown all afternoon
as we necked and fumbled in French
on a double-decker bus.
Jean-Paul carved our names on the back bench
with the date underneath. I was the girl
from a good suburb who longed to climb
the iron truss of the Eiffel Tower
a flag in my teeth and announce
something superb, something about
égalité and the yellow star
something about love, something about war.

May, 1966

Now I am in Paris, a stranger in two tongues
come to a bad hotel with a good address
where the Germans buffed their boots
with tags of huck towels and hung
their helmets from the curling gas jets
and dialed their home towns in Baden or Hesse.
I am the girl with her head full of heights
tutoying Jean-Paul in the blackout nights.
I see the Nazis under the arches
four abreast, thighs showy as birches.
The Nazis making water in the green urinal
at the Place de l'Etoile.
The Nazis making love in the Bois de Boulogne
a sea of used condoms.
The Nazis drinking their *bières*
at the Café de la Paix
fingering the same geraniums
the same concierge.

The girl that I was can see swastikas
lifting and swelling in the Place de la Concorde
where a blind and furious beggar, a purist

of a beggar with a bull's voice roars,
I am eighty years old and a *mutilé* of two wars!
For God's sake, you rich tourists,
open your purses!
I think I see Jean-Paul on crutches
on the rue de St. Honoré
and I hurry the other way
past a dozen little Jean-Pauls in shorts
so short as to beguile their innocent crotches
playing War in the Tuileries
boy-war, an international sport.

The fact is, I am the purist.
I cannot update to De Gaulle.
Police cars with sirens that bray
like donkeys in heat careen past
rightists and leftists, veterans of the Maquis
women, now wide-fronted matrons
whose heads were once shaved in public
Germans with Agfas, the Kodak Americans
the sad, the sane, the unfound.
Jean-Paul is not in the telephone book
not in Paris nor the outlying districts
for twenty kilometers around.

HISTORY LESSON

You were begotten in a vague war.
American planes ran their fingers
through the sky between truces
as your daddy crossed parallels
to plant you bald as an onion
in 1954.

Two years later you sailed
(you think you remember)
on a converted troopship full
of new wives and wet pants while
the plum pits of your mother's eyes
wobbled and threatened to come loose.

After that there were knots
in your father's GI work boots
and the sounds of night robbers
ransacking the rooming house
cantering up the staircase
to his delicate Korean lady.
You were six years into English
subtitles when they whisked her
away in a bedroll of lipsticks
and false eyelashes.

Before disasters there are omens.
Comets come, the geese lay bloody eggs.
In this case, the landlady tattled
alarm and sent for the cops.
She boiled saltines in blue milk
—a whiff of scald that still gags you—
until they came with red wristbones
and let you play games with the handcuffs
all the way to the stale clothes of state schools
Lysol washrooms and tin-tray suppers.

It is true that we lie down on cowflops
praying they'll turn into pillows.
It is true that our mothers explode
out of the snowballs of dreams
or speak to us down the chimney
saying our names above the wind
or scrape their legs like crickets
in the dead grass behind the toolshed
tapping a code we can't read.

That a man may be free of his ghosts
he must return to them like a garden.
He must put his hands in the sweet rot
uprooting the turnips, washing them
tying them into bundles
and shouldering the whole load to market.

DESPAIR

is a mildewed tent. Under the center pole
you must either bend double or take to your knees.
And suppose, after all that tugging and smoothing, you ease
yourself, blind end first, into your blanket roll—
wet under, and over, wool scratch, and you lying still,
lashed down for the season, hands tucked between your thighs,
the canvas stink in your nose, the night in your eyes—
what makes you think that rattling your ribs here will
save you? Camper, you are a bone-sore fool.
Somewhere a brown moth beats at a lighted window.
Somewhere a barn owl fastens into his mouse.
The ground heaves up its secret muster of toadstools.
They are marching to bear you away to the dumb show.
Yank up the pegs and come back! Come back in the house.

LAKE BUENA VISTA, FLORIDA, JUNE 16, 1987

Death claimed today from hummocks lost
to Cape Canaveral the last
pure dusky seaside sparrow
whose coastal range to its cost
was short and narrow.
A six-inch skulker in the matted grass
plain brown, no song to speak of but a trill
a bird hardly remarkable
was nullifed by rocket blasts.

How simply symbols replace habitat!
Tomorrow we will put it on a stamp
a first-day cover with Schaus swallowtail
the unmourned Key Largo rat
and fifty others sucked into the swamp
of extinction dredged by the human race.
The tower frames at Aerospace
quiver in the flush of another shot.

REMEMBERING PEARL HARBOR
AT THE TUTANKHAMEN EXHIBIT

Wearing the beard of divinity, King Tut
hunts the hippopotamus of evil.
He cruises the nether world on the back
of a black leopard. And here he has put
on his special pectoral, the one
painted with granulated gold. This will
adorn him as he crosses over.

       I shuffle
in line on December seventh to see
how that royal departure took place.
A cast of thousands is passing this way.
No one looks up from the alabaster
as jets crisscross overhead. Our breaths
cloud the cases that lock in the gold
and lapis lazuli.

       The Day
of Infamy, Roosevelt called it. I was
a young girl listening to the radio
on a Sunday of hard weather. Probably
not one in seven packed in these rooms
goes back there with me.

Implicit
throughout this exhibit arranged
by Nixon and Sadat as heads of state
is an adamantine faith
in total resurrection.
Therefore the king is conveyed
with a case for his heart
and another magnificent
hinged apparatus, far too small,
for his intestines, all in place,
all considered retrievable

whereas if one is to be blown
apart over land or water
back into the Nothingness
that preceded light, it is better
to go with the simplest detail:
a cross, a dogtag,
a clamshell.

THE WAITING GAME

I remember they used to stand
a little shabby and shy, on downtown street corners
all winter, message in hand
hawking Armageddon, like licensed pornographers
except for the eyes,
except for the bland believing smile, hellfire
certain in earthly disguise
stalking the city where *Jesus is coming: prepare!*

People said: cranks. Paranoids.
Some put a hand out for the pamphlet
and thought, Christ! How the unemployed
employ You Who do not keep the most
important final date,
making lying messiahs of the lost
who suffer You late,
who stand in breadlines, dreaming You their host.

But times have changed. The furtive pink-nosed bands
grown more assured on fear and hate
now smile crisply on the unredeemed,
sing doom in overcoats
canvass the suburbs where the air is clearer
although the word's the same

coercing commuters that the end is nearer
in the waiting game

and well-fed, block by block, for all one knows
they dread themselves the day the trumpet blows.

MOTHER ROSARINE

Next-door Mother Rosarine
of the square white front and black buckram
tugged up the morning with cinches of keys
rode through the Mass, a bristle-chinned queen
jingling the tongues that unlocked the linens
the larder, the gym suits that luffed at the knees
of the boarders, and swung on the door to His kingdom

through which I did not dare pass.
I came in screw curls and dotted swisses
came through the hedge to that swaddled lap.
Cheeks on her starch, a traitor to my class
I nibbled Christ's toes on the rosewood cross
and begged her, Mother, take off your cap.
Oh I filled up my vestal with earnest kisses.

Wrong, born wrong for the convent games
I hunched on the sidelines beggar fashion.
My child, said Mother Rosarine
rooting for your side is a useful passion.
She led three cheers and a locomotive for the team.
Beet-red Sister Mary Clare, a victim
of rashes, refereed. She called for time.

At vespers, hot in my body still
I stole back in up the convent stairs
and sat alone with the varnished smell
of the scribbled desks, and dreamed of angels.
There were lids to pry in that chalkdust air.
A rosary strung with lacquer-black kernels
slid in my pocket. It polished my fingers.

The seeds grew wet in my palm. Going down
clicking the blessings I made my own
and testing the treads for creaks, I could hear
Mother Rosarine's voice turn the churn downstairs.
In the buttery sunset, in the beadroll mansion
her nuns, like rows of cows in their stanchions
softly mooing, were making the sounds of prayer.

REHABILITATION CENTER

In the good suburb, in the bursting season
their canes awag in the yellow day
the newly maimed mince back to danger.

Cave by cave they come to build their hearing
hard as fists against the jangling birds
the slipslop of car wheels, walls' mimicries

the hollow rebuttal of planes. Curbs curse them.
Puddles damn their simplicity. At lot lines
forsythia is a swipe across the face.

Under a wide sky let them cry now
to be coddled, misread a tree, blacken shins
or bark their knees on countermands.

The downgrade is uncertain for us all.

In time they will grow competent,
love us, test and correct, feel words
on their quiet skin, begin to light our lamps.

Six weeks and they will swing around these corners
grotesque and right, their appetites restored.
It is true the sun is only heat,

but distance, depth, doorsills
are ridged on their maps until
they know exactly where they are now.

I see their lockstep tight as lilac buds.

Rolled like a hero sandwich
unfurled over breakfast gives
weight, volume, gravitas
to the puffball bellies
of the world's waifs.

Mouthfuls of bad news
in with the cornflakes
Suez to Saigon
Prague to Biafra.
The bacon is warped as
the coffee as black as
the day of my father's death.

Sundays my father
hairs sprouting out of
the v of his pajamas
took in the sitdowns
Pinkertons Bundists
sipped up the Lend-Lease
under his mustache.

In with the hash browns
in with the double-yolked

once over lightly eggs
mouthfuls of bad news.
Nothing has changed, Poppa.
The same green suburban lawn.
The same fat life.

The same cabin, the same stone fireplace,
red oak blazing in its sooty bin
and just outside, the October trees on fire
in the same slant of the five o'clock sun.
In the rocking chair, Louise Bogan
girlish with company back then.
In the straight chair, theatrically puffing
our mentor, John Holmes, with pipe.
We three novices lined up on the lumpy cot
while water was coaxed to boil over the hot
plate and tea was served in the club
they would never never invite us to join
who signed the plaque above the hearth
as evidence of tenancy and worth.

I strain to read above the confident fire
names of the early great and almost great:
Rumer Godden, Padriac Colum
Nikolai Lopatnikoff,
too many pale ones gone to smudges.
Use a penknife, I advise my friend
then ink each letter for relief
—as if a name might matter
against the falling leaf.

THE MESSAGE

John Holmes 1904–1962

Not even Yeats's mediums rapping the table
in the cold-eyed room at midnight were able
to raise the veil and slip a message through.
But the dream persists in which a letter from you
waits for the postman. A cat burglar, meanwhile,
rifles your pockets in the old-fashioned tiled
bathroom at the blind end of the upstairs hall.
Whatever you might have said he wads up small,
swipes the loose change and flushes the evidence.
Dear John, the dream's at my expense.

Would it have pleased you that the *Times* obit
called you poet and teacher of poets,
and extra cops were ordered up the Hill
to steer the summery crowds who came to chapel?
We squared our backs obediently and chewed
on the gristle of reverent platitudes.
A man deserves to go out on his words:
It is my own death I count kisses toward,
you said in a snug old rhetoric, remote
from the gagging coal that closed your throat.

Thinking to slip my message past the bored
impersonal divider who stands guard,
I played three angry sets of tennis on
the afternoon we read you out of your bones.
I felt three blisters coming up at deuce
and popped them ceremonially for the juice,
insisting in a way you'd understand
on the Mosaic right to give my raw red hand
in penance for my own death left behind
unchosen, and to keep yours young in mind.

MAKING THE CONNECTION

Looking for good news to skate out on
over the pond of sleep, I'm tricked
instead to hear him whimpering in the kitchen.
His ghost comes in on metal toenails,
scratches himself, the thump of thighbone
on linoleum. Ghost laps water. Whines. Soon
he will howl aloud in the prison of his deafness
waking the grown children who all live elsewhere.

I sit up, breaking the connection
like hanging up on my brother.

I am ten. I go down terrified
past a houseful of bubbling breathers
unlatch the cellar door, go further
down in darkness to lie on old carpet
next to the incontinent puppy.
His heartbeat, my heartbeat comfort us
and the fluttering pulse of the furnace
starting up, stopping.

Brother, Brother Dog, is that who you were?
Is that who I was?

LATELY, AT NIGHT

Father,
lately I find myself repairing
at night by inches the patchwork of your death.
The undertaker's elevator
slides upstairs like a sneak thief
going hand over hand up a back drainpipe
to an unused bedroom. The french doors open
and unction takes me by the elbow.
I am pulled up short
between those two big boys your sons, my brothers
brave as pirates putting into
a foreign port.

Tonight again
you who had sworn off funerals
and said you'd have us send out for champagne
lie stuffed and stitched like a suckling pig
prettied up for the fiesta.
Even from the doorway your profile
sticks up against air and velvet like a cutaway
springing erect in a child's pop-out book.
The jut of your nose is a thumb forced backward.
Your eyes, those crafty Indians

are three-quarters closed, but the twig
you wait for doesn't snap
and the old odd cleft of your chin
is faintly blue under a brand-new shave.

We whisper over you, doing business:
the middle-priced blanket of flowers
the car to call for the reverend
organ music to muffle the heels of all comers
and for our mother's dizziness
two ushers to superintend.
But where are the belly dancers
the cake that breaks open
the whiskey and rattlers and three-corner party hats
and in this extravaganza
where is the gently tipsy old lady
who comes on at a foxtrot
whisking you under the archway and out
as simply as that?

I will tell them
you died with three days' whiskers on your face.
I will tell them

the final blip from the wires
daringly threaded into your heart
to keep the pace
announced itself on the radar screen
and faded down the track
one small plane easing itself over the horizon
and not the gas mask full of oxygen
and not the long shots of adrenaline
and nothing lusty left could haul you back.

Father,
lately at night as I watch your chest
to help it to breathe in
and swear it moves, and swear I hear the air
rising and falling
even in the dream it is my own fat lungs
feeding themselves, greedy as ever.
Smother, drown or burn, Father
Father, no more false moves, I beg you.
Back out of my nights, my dear dead undergroundling.
It is time. Let the pirates berth their ships
broach casks, unload the hold, and let
the dead skin of your forehead
be a cold coin under my lips.

III

BREAKTHROUGH: NONESUCH POND

This foreign land is where we swim in summer.
Three days and nights of freeze have caught it flat
so that the underbelly shows. A swimmer
hardly sees these fingerlings, or what
the bottom current twitches so that now
they look like fish among the magicked plants
fastened in layers of glass. Around we go
crisping the saucer sides. Sun and blue sky
have brought our neighbors out.

Medleys of skaters: girls with bells
tied to their laces for a mating call,
roving boys dodging, elastic as eels,
smacking pucks, tangling hockey sticks,
shucking their jackets off, squat
quilted wobblers, falling, hauled upright
by trousered mothers, tall and stiff as cranes.

Solitary men skating, hands behind
their backs, one puffing on a pipe and leaning
like a weathered sapling into the wind,
and always a skidding dog, cold, whining,
being collared by the boy who let him out.

Late afternoon. Skaters still seam a ring
around the pond. We know the center's thin—
a gray curd over black water where a spring
freshens the core—and keep away
but someone's child, chasing for a puck
shoots out beyond the mark and is snatched in.

No warning crack, no cry—and he is gone
or almost gone, except three boys slide flat
and make a chain and clamp a hockey stick
against his chest—and that is almost that
except the safe boy melts the skaters back.
The pond is clear. The afternoon runs out.

Tonight will be enough to mend the break
so that, on this flat plain, no flag
will mark tomorrow where the boy went down.
Let skaters, circling this deceptive skim,
know here the ice uncorks. From this line
days will eat the crust off, cattails
in the shallows sprout new stems
and the jellied spring spawn hatch.
Nights enough will bring the peepers out.

JUNIOR LIFE SAVING

Isosceles of knees
my boys and girls sit
cross-legged in blue July
and finger the peel
of their sun-killed skin
or pick at the splintery boards
of the dock. The old lake
smiles to a fish
and quiets back to glass.

Class, I say, this is
the front head release.
And Adam's boy, whose ribs
dance to be numbered aloud
I choose to strangle me.
Jaw down in his embrace
I tell the breakaway.
Now swimming in the air
we drown, wrenching the chin,
clawing the arm around.

The magic seeps away.
My heroes frown to see
a menace in the element

they lately loved.
Class, I say (and want
to say, children, my dears,
I too know how to be afraid)
I tell you what I know:
go down to save.

Now two by two they leave
the dock to play at death
by suffocation.
The old lake smiles,
turned sudden to a foe
taking my children down
half held by half
ordaining they let go.

IN THAT LAND

Hungry for oysters to suck down with gin
we go at sunset and low water when
the sea returns our backyard, scrubbed but stinking.
In an abundance of dying, crabs bleach out
their whiskery legs, and fields of minnows stiffen.
The shell of a horseshoe crab is the Kaiser's helmet
I swing by the tail till the natural glue lets go.

We walk in the shallows where stones become oysters
older than stones, grown in on each other
lip over lip, greasy with algae, to cover
the eyeball we eat. Until we unlock the joints,
alive. Alive perhaps as we swallow.
We are the oyster killers who live in a world
of sundown and gin and shellfish within our means.

At night the sound of water rocks our bed.
The chowder moon is a bowl of milky clams.
And as we lie in a tangle of stars and pines,
hardshell beetles blunder against the screen,
roll on their backs and die, cracking like popcorn.

By the hall light that pulls the June bugs down
I see your legs walk past me to the window.

Your buttocks are two moons tipped on their cradles.
Your back, a new tent arching. Snakes sit
in the bulge of your arms, their tongues your elbows.

The big bed smells of salt. When you come back
I move from my own cocoon to wind in yours.
Inside my eyes I count the shapes of shells,
the armor of broken beetles, mismatched halves
of oysters, the calico tops of scalded crabs.

I will not count our own small gift of bones.
We hold ourselves in one world at a time.

ROUND TRIP

Missionaries at the ferry slip
girding up for island outposts
carrying their right gods with them—
dogs cats parakeets air mattresses
rods reels creels an extra coffeepot—
their habits starched, their countenances gray
meet perfect Christians coming the other way
carrying their right gods with them—
dogs cats parakeets air mattresses
rods reels creels an extra coffeepot
periwinkles pockmarked driftwood
skate egg cases brittle starfish
smelling faintly of decay—
meet missionaries coming the other way.

REMEMBERING YOU

Skiing the mountain alone
on a day of difficult moods
with snowflakes of rottenstone
at the liverish altitudes

and the bones of the birches pale
as milk and the humpbacked spine
of an untouched downhill trail
turned suddenly serpentine

a day comes into my head
when we rose by aerial tram
bubbles strung on a thread
of a mobile diagram

rose to the mountain's crest
on a day of electric blue
and how, my enthusiast,
I made the descent with you,

the beautiful greed of our run
taken on edge, tiptoe
with a generous spill of sun
on the toytown roofs below

as on powder side by side
running lightly and well
we lipped and took the untried
easily parallel.

GRACE

Hens have their gravel. Gravel sticks
The way it should stick, in the craw.
And stone on stone is tooth
For grinding raw.

And grinding raw, I learn from this
To fill my crop the way I should.
I put down puddingstone
And find it good.

I find it good to line my gut
With tidy octagons of grit.
No loophole and no chink
Make vents in it.

And in it vents no slime or sludge.
No losses sluice, no terrors slough.
God, give me appetite
For stone enough.

THE APPOINTMENT

This is my wolf. He sits
at the foot of the bed
in the dark all night

breathing so evenly
I am almost deceived.
It is not the swollen

cat uncurling
restlessly, a house
of kittens knocking

against her flanks.
It isn't the hot fog
fingering the window locks

while the daffodils
wait in the wings
like spearholders.

Not the children fisted
in three busy dreams
they will retell at breakfast

and not you, clearly
not you beside me
all these good years

that he watches.
I lie to him nightlong.
I delay him with praises.

In the morning we wash
together chummily.
I rinse my toothbrush.

After that
he puts his red eyes out
under the extra blanket.

POEM FOR MY SON

Where water laps my hips
it licks your chin. You stand
on tiptoe looking up
and swivel on my hands.
We play at this and laugh,
but understand you weigh
now almost less than life
and little more than sea.
So fine a line exists
between buoyance and stone
that, catching at my wrists,
I feel love notch the bone
to think you might have gone.

To think they smacked and pumped
to squall you into being
when you swam down, lungs limp
as a new balloon, and dying.
Six years today they bent
a black tube through your chest.
The tank hissed in the tent.
I leaned against the mast
outside that sterile nest.

And now inside the sea
you bump along my arm,
learning the narrow way
you've come from that red worm.
I tell you, save your air
and let the least swell ease you.
Put down, you flail for shore.
I cannot bribe nor teach you
to know the wet will keep you.

And cannot tell myself
unfasten from the boy.
On the Atlantic shelf
I see you wash away
to war or love or luck,
prodigious king, a stranger.
Times I stepped on a crack
my mother was in danger,
and time will find the chinks
to work the same in me.
You bobbled in my flanks.
They cut you from my sea.
Now you must mind your way.

Once, after a long swim
come overhand and wheezy
across the dappled seam
of lake, I foundered, dizzy,
uncertain which was better:
to fall there and unwind
in thirty feet of water
or fight back for the land.
Life would not let me lose it.
It yanked me by the nose.
Blackfaced and thick with vomit
it thrashed me to my knees.
We only think we choose.

But say we choose. Pretend it.
Your wrist's blue pulse demands
you heed the call to spend it
throbbing against the bone.
Swim off, swim off alone.

MAGELLAN STREET, 1974

This is the year you fall in
love with the Bengali poet
and the Armenian bakery stays open
Saturday nights till eleven
across the street from your sunny
apartment with steep fo'c'sle stairs
up to an attic bedroom.
Three-decker tenements flank you.
Cyclone fences enclose
flamingos on diaper-size lawns.

This is the year, in a kitchen
brightened with pots of basil
and mint, I see how
your life will open, will burst from
the maze in its walled-in garden
and streak toward the horizon.
Your pastel maps lie compliant
on the counter as we stand here
not quite up to exchanging
our day books, our night thoughts
and burn the first batch of
chocolate walnut cookies.

Of course you move on,
my circumnavigator.
Tonight as I cruise past your corner
a light goes on in a window.
Two shapes sit at a table.

THE KNOT

Lately, I am changing houses like sneakers and socks.
Time zones wrinkle off me casually.
There's a row of borrowed kitchens, look-alikes
in which I crack the eggs and burn the toast
but even in Danville, Kentucky, my ghosts
relocate as easily as livestock
settling into another fraternity.

Angel of my *cafard*, displaced daughter, it was
an out-of-season snow we walked in
dreamy as soothsayers in the Ardennes,
where the World War I monuments, Adonises
and sloe-eyed angels, softened with verdigris,
have been updated with the names of all
those who died in labor camps
or up against the wall.

At Bastogne the wind mourned from the swamp.
A giant alarm clock ticked in the Hall
of the States, half Parthenon,
half Stonehenge, hugely American
and here I was the least at home
of all the alien places, alien beds
in the presence of my generation's dead.

I swim in the college pool to put down the *cafard*.
At 82 degrees, it's mother-warm
and the coach, a silent giant, calls me Ma'am.
He apologizes that the water is cloudy.
O my chlorinated Mediterranean, hold me!
I rock across that cradle for twenty laps
then haul myself back into the freight of my body.

Back in the antebellum manse where a diamond bit
the glass to say the owner's name, Sam McKee,
I study a snapshot of us standing in a Brussels park,
the sky all lightstruck. Out of those streaks
there thunders the horse that kicked you in the cheek
when you were twelve. The welt raised up as round
as a biscuit. We had no ice but put a frozen steak to it.
Still, I see the scar come up in certain lights.

Let the joists of this house endure their dry rot,
let termites abide in their blind tunnels.
I chew on the knot
we were once. Your eyes, serene
in the photo, look thoughtfully out
and could be bullet holes, or beauty spots.

THE ARCHAEOLOGY OF A MARRIAGE

When Sleeping Beauty wakes up
she is almost fifty years old.
Time to start planning her retirement cottage.
The Prince in sneakers stands thwacking
his squash racket. He plays with the guys
at his club. It gets the heart action up.
What *he* wants in the cottage
is a sauna and an extra-firm Beauty-
rest mattress, which *she* sees as an exquisite
sarcasm directed against her long slumber.
Was it her fault he took so long to
hack his way through the brambles?
Why didn't he carry a chainsaw
like any sensible woodsman?
Why, for that matter, should any
intelligent modern woman
have to lie down at the prick of
a spindle etcetera etcetera
and he is stung to reply in kind
and soon they are at it.

If only they could go back to
the simplest beginnings. She
remembers a blurry snapshot

of herself in a checked gingham outfit.
He is wearing his Navy dress whites.
She remembers the illicit weekend
in El Paso twenty years before
illicit weekends came out of the closet.
Just before Hiroshima, just before Nagasaki
they nervously fondled each other
he an ensign on a forged three-day pass
she a technical virgin from Boston.
What he remembers is vaster:
something about his whole future
compressed to a stolen weekend.
He was to have shipped out tomorrow
for the massive land intervention.
He was to have stormed Japan.
Then, merely thinking of dying
gave him a noble erection.

Now, thanatopsis is calmer,
the first ripe berry on the stem
leading his greedy hands deeper
into the thicket than he has ever been.
Deeper than he cares to go.
At the sight of the castle, however

he recovers his wits and backtracks
meanwhile picking. Soon his bucket
is heavier etcetera than ever
and he is older etcetera and still
no spell has been recast back at
Planned Acres Cottage.
Every day he goes forth to gather
small fruits. Each evening she stands
over the stewpot skimming
acid foam from the jam
expecting to work things out
awaiting, you might say, a unicorn,
the slotted spoon in her hand.

IV

THE EAR

It is a very old story my Mafia-Tony tells
which begins in the North End with a drunken father
and eleven sisters and brothers, and swells

to the night of the razor which carried away,
cleanly, the spiral top half of his right ear.
He is my fruit man. I call here each Saturday.

I see the Christopher medal that sits
in the black mat of his chest. I inspect
the bananas, the melons and cherries, the pits

of avocados building to trees in their pots
on the south-facing shelf over the money drawer.
They are as sunny and safe as Tony is not

when he talks, with the fire of fathers, about
his daughter. This is his only daughter. He pays
her husband good money to mind, it turns out,

one of the several stands that Tony owns.
This one he keeps by himself out of sentiment.
It was the first. A man needs to stand alone.

The son-in-law, seven-time planter of fruit
in the womb of the daughter, rankles in Father's accounts.
But most of the money is not in this kind of an outfit,

Tony confides. There are three convents near here
to which he tenders in quantity and at a reverent profit
the best he can bargain at auction for the good Sisters.

For the Sisters who raise up the young in the way they should go;
for the Sisters who govern the sick and reign over women in labor;
for the Sisters whose business it is to pray for us all below.

Tony cuts me a grapefruit from Texas. The pink spokes
are outlined in white; there are three white seeds in the heart.
As he talks, I can see his nuns, all Ingres' Odalisques,

who, having pledged with Christ, ought now to be faithful
to gristle and narrow beds, recumbent and at ease instead
inside their habits. For them, dark plums flown from Brazil,

kumquats and currants loosed from their leaves in the sun,
Bosc pears and Anjous for them, and small tangerines that will
slip from their skins at the nick of a nail of a nun.

I see them dipping red berries in sugar and telling them,
like beads. They are blackbirds in perfect Byzantium
being fed by Nubian eunuchs on their knees. Amid *Te Deums*

rise visions of guava and pomegranate when Tony calls.
They are blessed with casabas and mangoes and over them all
hangs an icon shaped like Tony's lost ear, on the wall.

THE DIARY KEEPER

in memory of T. H. White

I speak to the loneliness of the diary keeper
holing up for months at a time
in his cottage abutting a haybarn, where
the valley folk appear below like black fleas
in the snow, and the grouse rattle up
in a flurry of extra heartbeats.

In phrases lazy as marriage
he confides that the dogs have run down a deer,
the pipes in the kitchen are frozen
but the fire comes forth each morning,
leather softens, spring is a dazzling absence
and later, the bitch has whelped too soon.
I drowned seven, I won't exorcise
this shame with words, but feel it.

I would speak to the man turned inward
mending and making do.
He pries words up out of Latin,
patches a flannel shirt and wishes
for *a sewing machine, an auto-giro,*
the Oxford English Dictionary

all the while throwing up bridges
across his God-fired rages,
griefs smothered under the coal scuttle,
guilts laid over the long winter drunks,
the carouses, the sick melancholic forenoons.

The reader I am is given
like him to the winter habit of thinking.
On a day when the snow flies all cross-eyed
and the woodstove spits out its caulkings
and scattering hay to the horses, the pitchfork
raises a fieldmouse on one prong,

I follow him into the heart of his kitchen,
the ferment of his bachelor salvages
to say that I too *would be more of*
a coward if I had the courage
and coward, come muffled,
come gaitered, come waving
a fifth of Kilkenny Irish
to mourn him into his due date.

THE LOVERS LEAVE BY SEPARATE PLANES

She is going back
to the cash register of an old marriage.
He sees her ringing up days
letting the drawer fly open
on her half-grown sons
and breaking the rolls of nickels and dimes
into their proper dividers.

She thinks of him tomorrow at his desk
exploring an old translation
prying apart the brittle glue
between two languages to take out words.
She sees him lecturing gently to
an amphitheater of students
all of them taking useful notes.

Meanwhile the lovers have climbed into
the same sky, going east and west.
Clouds solid as the Arctic Pole billow
beneath them. Whole counties of ice floes
are underfoot. At this point
the appearance of polar bears
would not surprise him
one holding a walleyed fish in its paws
one chewing the flipper of a stranded seal.

For that matter she is prepared
to see him well booted and fur capped
icicles in his beard striding over the snowfield
breaking through gauze and violet gels
running abreast to knock at her window.
They would tell each other.
They would speak in large gestures
like deaf mutes
keeping nothing inside.

Up attic, Lucas Harrison, God rest
his frugal bones, once kept a tidy account
by knifecut of some long-gone harvest.
The wood was new. The pitch ran down to blunt
the year: 1811, the score: 10, he carved
into the center rafter to represent
his loves, beatings, losses, hours, or maybe
the butternuts that taxed his back and starved
the red squirrels higher up each scabbed tree.
1812 ran better. If it was bushels he risked,
he would have set his sons to rake them ankle deep
for wintering over, for wrinkling off their husks
while downstairs he lulled his jo to sleep.

By 1816, whatever the crop goes sour.
Three tallies cut by the knife are all
in a powder of dead flies and wood dust pale as flour.
Death, if it came then, has since gone dry and small.

But the hermit makes this up. Nothing is known
under this rooftree keel veed in with chestnut
ribs. Up attic he always hears the ghosts
of Lucas Harrison's great trees complain
chafing against their mortised pegs,

a woman in childbirth pitching from side to side
until the wet head crowns between her legs
again, and again she will bear her man astride
and out of the brawl of sons he will drive like oxen
tight at the block and tackle, whipped to the trace,
come up these burly masts, these crossties broken
from their growing and buttoned into place.

Whatever it was is now a litter of shells.
Even at noon the attic vault is dim.
The hermit carves his own name in the sill
that someone after will take stock of him.

Sundowning,
the doctor calls it, the way
he loses words when the light fades.
The way the names of his dear ones
fall out of his eyeglass case.
Even under the face of his father
in an oval on the wall
he cannot say *Catherine, Vera, Paul*
but goes on loving them out of place.
Window, wristwatch, cup, knife
are small prunes that drop from his pockets.
Terror sweeps him from room to room.
Knowing how much he weighed once
he knows how much he has departed his life.
Especially he knows how the soul
can slip out of the body unannounced
like that helium-filled balloon
he opened his fingers on, years back.

Now it is dark. He undresses
and takes himself off to bed
as loose in his skin as a puppy,
afraid the blankets will untuck,
afraid he will flap up, unblessed.

Instead, proper nouns return to his keeping.
The names of faces are put back
in his sleeping mouth. At first light
he gets up, grateful once more
for how coffee smells. Sits stiff
at the bruised porcelain table
saying them over, able to
with only the slightest catch.
Coffee. Coffee cup. Watch.

THE YOUNG INSTRUCTOR
IN A WINTER LANDSCAPE

As though a campus might become
effete without one
there is always a hill to climb.
Harvard alone
in all New England hurries
on the level
but there traffic purifies
the intellectual.
Hills are warm work in icy weather.
Something the mind
can chew on, piecing together
a way around
slick patches, worrying in the throat
of great bells
pushing past, wrong way, the not-yet
panic bars, down halls
to classroom doors that time has torn
the message from
leaving the stain, perhaps, of 14
in dim monogram.
Smiling at old men who taught
him once (he does
this out of choice or habit
or is virtuous)

crossing the magic circle, smelling
chalk dust, lipstick
printer's ink, yeasty ideas, wet woolens
reading hieroglyphs
left on the walls from the last class
(all he knows
he does not know: Russian or calculus)
opening a window
on that all-climbing hill of Sisyphus
he sees it has begun to snow
and all the faces facing him are his.

so kneed and knived
by students extracting the metaphor
let me forget to nibble at
whose ax you borrowed, on which date
you went to jail, who paid the tax
and blink instead to see you stump
out in thick night, Concord to hut
a bag of rye meal on your shoulder
guessing your route between tight-fitted
pines as through the narrowest sort
of doorway with a blind man's wit.
Thoreau, that kind of boldness moves me.

I like you best brazening out
alternatives. One day you are
a hoecake vegetarian
and proud to chew on purslane weed
the next, so savage you could spit
a Mexican or fry a rat
or get raw woodchuck down, savoring
its musk.
       I bless your curses on
all tillage that requires more
than a day's work for a month of bread.
Swearing and sweating in your own cause

until you came to say it was
not beans you hoed, nor you that hoed
them in the stony rows, I see
you moving close and mindlessly
to loving the backbreak of yourself.

And loving the blueprint that you make
of ice fits, loon chase, water tables—
safeminded ponderer—
        you tell
me you could sprawl across the seats
of your wide-hipped sensible dory
and drift all forenoon till the bow
grating on sand awoke you to
another shore. Whatever branch
cut in the blue face of the world
you saw from that hard hot saddle
it was the same tree, and your own
dry skin in the stolid boat
as if that pond were meant for oars
and plumb-line measurements.
        We are
least likely kin in this: I planned
to read that you could loll, legs curled
like fishes' tails under the belly

of a razor-keel canoe, one hand
on the near thwart above, until
the lake soaked you in two and only
your head was real or dry.
        Or that
you could raise a chorus over
astonished fishes, bob for a mile
or swamp your rib house in one jump
pulling it over you for a blind
and drift in that pond-lapped airhole
dark as the underside of eyelids
fastened in night, losing and finding
the sign of your wily loon, the hollow
voice of your breath, the hard lines of
your floating hips.
        Instead, I test
and love you for brave cowardice
in the graceless skiff
in the tightening woodland
in the tall bean patch

in life near the bone,
almost true and gone.

GOING TO JERUSALEM

Bedecked with scapulars
heavy with huge crosses
and crying out abroad
Death to the Infidel!
the Franks swept by in waves
riding their stone horses
big-barreled stallions
deemed brave enough for battle

only to meet the swart
small mustachioed Turks
crouched nimbly athwart
their slight Arabian mares
the only gender they
thought fit for close combat

and thus the Rhenish stones
running amok among
the little dish-faced mares
the high-tailed swans-necked mares
begetting as they went
plunged the entire Crusade
upon the Eastern Front
into chaotic bliss.

Angels from streets of gold
benignly looked on this
God's wonder to behold.
Both sides stood by unhorsed
while Nature ran its course.

HAMAN'S EARS

Notice this time again how the Jew comes in, in disguise:
Moses, floating on rushes in the Nile's muddy backwash
and now at this season, Esther, Esther of the sloe eyes
warned by her worried uncle to hold back her origins.

It is almost spring. I take down the Book
and I read how Ahasuerus put away Vashti his queen
for something unspecified (she did not come when he
    beckoned).
And after the lady was banished, his royal wrath pricking him
    still

the King sent couriers out for virgins that he could pluck.
And here in the wings waits Esther (I am reading out of the
    Book),
a maiden of beautiful form and fair to look on.

That was in Persia, five centuries, as they say in the temple
before the common era. And in Shushan the castle
it was a golden time of bounty measured in marble
in cords of fine linen and purple, and bickering concubines.

The rest happens quickly. You can read it there for yourself.
It makes me think of John's head on a platter. We eat these
    pastries
which were, in my childhood, called Haman's ears.

I suppose that the devil has ears like Pan's, and cloven hoofs
and canters about with the leer of a satyr.
I learn, but too late to destroy the image, that *tashen*

means pockets. Dustmen's pockets, I think, or the mailman's
pouch. And in it, a secret edict wangled out of the King:
wipe out the Jews. They are too proud to bow down.

Esther, that happy know-nothing, begs Mordecai to get dressed.
Why do you tear up your tunic? Why do you lie down in dirt?
And even after he tells her, poor uncle, he has to blackmail her.
Why should she rescue her people, except to save her own skin?
She didn't ask for the part, this reluctant heroine.

In Sunday School there is a party, something like Hallowe'en.
The girls dress up as Esther, the passionate Queen
anointed to come into his presence, and jeweled, but shy
and every small boy is the King.
No one wants to wear sackcloth and worry like Mordecai.
After all, he is only the uncle, he has his troubles.

And unlike that night of spirits, filled up with witches and satans
no little American Jew wants to be Haman.
As the story is told them, the children have shakers they rattle

to drown out so much as the sound of his name.
I have not heard my children question, as it is written:
the Jews smote all their enemies with the stroke of the sword

and did what they would unto those that hated them.
Seventy and five thousand they slew. And Haman's ten sons
—for the sins of the father are so visited—they hanged
on the gallows. I do not read them this message.

The evening is merry. We lounge at the supper table.
I say it is time for dessert and pass round the *hamantashen.*
After all, after all, what do the children know?

That the King was a good man, rich, strong and noble
and Haman, well, he was a nazi and what Esther did was good.
Even in Persia, in perfumes and bangles and silk stuff
she remembered that she was a Jew.
They know enough.

FOR ANNE AT PASSOVER

I

Cold Easter week and the hard buds forming, shake
their mitre caps at me. The tower bells
sing Christly sweet and everywhere
new scents—honey and blood—work the air.

My students, outside the college halls, regroup,
share notes, and smoke. Coats open, no hats, no gloves.
Some metabolic principle
keeps them warm enough until the bell.
Or love. Or thoughts of going home. Time now,
we mind the syllabus that juxtaposes
Socrates, inviting the poison cup
saying *there is no fear that it will stop*
with me, and Jesus, apportioning His week
however accidentally, with our Greek.

A kind of water-walking, Socrates
goes barefoot and uncaring over ice
stands tranced through two dawns, is able
to drink all comers underneath the table
and takes no lover in his night
except philosophy, *that dear delight*.

In air heavy as damask roses we read
the prison scene together. The weather abets us
and a great pocking rain commences.
We smell resurgence prickling our senses.

Son and sage hear voices. They keep no books,
but loose disciples on the world to tell
their missions, miracles, and choices:
in Christ's name, Joan burns for her voices.
In Christ's name shunned, historic news
the Jews their own stoned Jew refuse.

And Socrates, messiah true or false
how might the Christ have come to take our sins
without you, *terribly at ease in Zion*?
You die now, for no man and in no pain,
bathed and bedded according to the fashion,
friends who see you out your only Passion.
No nails, excepting as the soul is hung
against the flesh till death unfasten it.
One student says you sinned the sin of pride.
Another consecrates your suicide.

I say myths knit the world up when men die
for love, and if they lie, love needs the lie.
Time now. In Holy Week the tower bell
returns us to a faithful Friday rain.
Baggage and books, my students move about,
wish me a happy Easter, and go out.

II

Home by subway, I dare to see
my eye stare in my eye
and black it out
and see my head, which best of all
I thought I knew
elongate, squash or disengage
itself, swim off and leave
my motiveless shoulders
lost in doubt.

Still, I get out
uptown, as decorous as the next
feel useful in the buildings
out of habit
peer through a window
at fat chocolate rabbits

and price Madonna lilies
and buy an egg
with a crystal candy scene
inside—a peephole
for the eye of a child—
and look before I eat
and put up my umbrella
in the three o'clock street.

They have unpinned Him in the rain.
Cabs spin from St. Philip's
and cars unpark
and I walk where disbelief
clacks at my soul,
an old god in my pocket
worrying the hole.
Now all the saving bells begin.
I could not make Him to unmake my sin.

III
Tonight, the damask cloth laid, the loving cup
brimmed with sweet wine, I think of those my kin
who sat that Friday, inviting Elijah in
and swore he never came, nor comes again.

I think of Judas, the prophecy fetched up
to truth at our mutual season: yours to seek
your pierced and honored Son in the dim cave
and sing *resurgam,* drink His winey life
         there at the rail for pity's sake
         redeem yourself, all men, as if
there were still time in this hard-budding time

and mine to mind another book, remind
my blood relations we are marked in the blood
of an earlier lamb, and call God good
Who thumped our Moses so to send us out
and turned aside and hardened Pharaoh's heart
         ten times, Antagonist! to put
         us on that dusty pathway through
Your brackish sea. So we come to praise You.

Yearly, the youngest child, asking why
this night is different from all other nights
is told, his mouth absorbing bittersweets,
the bondage years in Egypt, and in some way
learns to perpetuate them from that day.
I remember my father's mother boiled
chickens with their feet on and we ate,

blasphemous modern children, from her plate
both meat and milk and stayed up loved and late
no letter law applying to a child.
I have sealed her in me, her fierce love
    of kindred all she had to give
    and my drowned Polish ancestry
washed out of Europe, rises up in me.

We pray tonight, dip herbs and pour out wine
forever what we are. I hear the rain
swelling the hard buds, all our fetishes
the simple sum of promises or wishes:
a radioactive rain in Pakistan
and Haifa, Yucca Flats, the Vatican,
    on all my kind: Manhattan rich
    or Yemen poor, who break flat bread
tonight and bless their newly buried dead.

What do we do, who eat to celebrate
with Eucharist and matzoh each man's fate?
I take a funny comfort reading how
Bakongo tribes, hard on the pulsing spew
of the afterbirth, would kiss that cord

and tuck it in the belly of their god
      so that its navel bud protrudes
      where we are mewling, swathed to hold
our button fast. We die, that knob unsealed.

Now God forgive us where we live
the ways we love are relative.
Yours, Anne, the sacramental arts
that divide Him in three parts.
Mine, the vengeful King of pride
despite Whose arm his children died.
Theirs, the dance, the drums that throb
who bless the statue's belly knob.

Guests of our gods, slaves to our origins
we pray and eat tonight in greening weather.
Time swells the buds. A sharper rain begins
wetting us all who suck at love together.

1984: THE POET VISITS EGYPT AND ISRAEL

Sand, sand. In the university the halls,
seats, tabletops, sills, are gritty with it.
Birds fly in and out of the open windows.
She speaks, amplified, on American
women poets since World War One
to an audience familiar with Dickinson,
Poe, and at a safe remove, Walt Whitman.

Afterward, thick coffee in thimbles. Sticky cakes
with the faculty. Nothing is said that could trespass
on her status as guest from another, unveiled life.
She is a goddess, rich, white, American
and a Jew. It says so in some of her poems.

There are no visible Jews in the American
Embassy, nor at the Cultural Center.
The one synagogue, beige stucco, asleep
in the Sabbath sun, is shuttered tight
and guarded by languid soldiers with bayonets.

All that she cannot say aloud: the congruities
of bayonets and whips; starved donkeys
and skeletal horses pulling impossible loads;
the small, indomitable Egyptian flies

that perch on lips, settle around the eyes
and will not be waved away.

Transported between lectures she arrives
at the Sheraton, which sits apart in an oasis.
Outdoors in the sports enclave, pool attendants
in monogrammed turtlenecks, like prep-school athletes,
carry iced salvers from bar to umbrellaed table,
proffer thick towels, reposition chaises longues
for the oiled, bikinied, all-but-naked bodies
of salesmen's wives and airline attendants on holdover.

What do they think about, she wonders,
as they glide among the infidels, these men
whose own wives wrap up head to toe in public,
whose uncles and cousins creep from day to day
in a state of chronic low-grade emergency.

Anonymous again in transit,
she leaves for Tel Aviv at night.
El Al's flight, a frail umbilicus
that loops three times a week to the Holy Land,
is never posted on the Departures Board.
The takeoff's dodgy, as if in fear of flak,

as if God once again might turn aside
and harden Pharaoh's heart, fill up the sea.

Once down, she knows the desert by its garden,
the beachfront by its senior citizens
assembled for calisthenics on the sand.
An hour later in the Old City
she sees a dozen small white donkeys,
descendants of the one that Jesus straddled,
trot docilely beside Volkswagen Beetles.

She peers into archaeological digs that reach
through limestone down to the days of Babylon,
pridefully down to the first tribes of Yahweh
sacrificing scapegoats on a stone.
Down through the rubble of bones and matter
—Constantinian, Herodian, Hasmonean—
that hold up our contemporary clutter.

In a restored Burnt House from A.D. 70,
the year the Romans sacked the second Temple,
she dutifully clambers down to view
scorch marks, gouged walls, some human bones
and a troop of army recruits on tour.

At the Western Wall, Sephardic Jews,
their genders separated by a grill,
clap for the bar mitzvah boy with spit curls
who struggles to lift a gold-encrusted Torah
that proclaims today he is a man.

Near the Via Dolorosa, among the schlock
for sale—amber beads, prayer rugs, camel saddles—
lamb legs are offered, always with one testicle
attached. Ubiquitous sweet figs, olive trees
botanically certified to be sprouts
from the sacred roots of Gethsemane.

A man whose concentration-camp tattoo
announces he was zero six nine eight
picks through a tangle of ripe kumquats
beside a Bedouin, her hands and face daubed blue,
who could as easily have been a Druid,
the poet thinks, and she an early Christian.

Meanwhile, clusters of Hasidic zealots
—most of them recent Brooklyn imports—
in bobbing dreadlocks and stovepipe hats
pedal breakneck on ten-speed bikes along
the claustral streets of the Arab Quarter

to await the messianic moment any minute
now. Look for a pillar of fire and in it
the one true Blessed-be-He, whose very name
cannot be spoken in the waiting game.

The one true Blessed-be-He, who is still hidden.
Parental discretion was advised for viewing
news clips of Syrian shock troops, soldiers
holding live snakes, biting them on command
chewing and spitting out the raw flesh, reciting
In this way we will chew and spit out the enemy.
As if the young in these geographies had not
yet heard of torture, frag bombs, the crying
out at night that is silenced by garrotte.

How will it end, she wonders, in the name
of God, in the name of all gods revving up
to this high-pitched hum, like tripwire
stretched taut before the spark ignites the fuse
fragmenting life for life, blood running
in the streets to mingle Shiite, Druse,
Israeli, French, American.
If I forget thee, O Jerusalem,
may my right hand forget its cunning.

ABOUT THE AUTHOR

MAXINE KUMIN is the author of thirteen books of poems, most recently *The Long Marriage, Connecting the Dots,* and *Looking for Luck;* a memoir entitled *Inside the Halo and Beyond: Anatomy of a Recovery;* three essay collections; a collection of short stories; four novels; and an animal-rights murder mystery. She has received numerous awards, including the Aiken Talyor Prize, the Poets' Prize, the Ruth E. Lilly Poetry Prize, and the Pulitzer Prize (in 1973) for *Up Country,* her fourth book of poems. She served as Consultant in Poetry to the Library of Congress before that post was renamed Poet Laureate of the United States, and as Poet Laureate of New Hampshire form 1989 to 1994. She has taught at numerous colleges and universities, including Princeton, Columbia, Brandeis, MIT, and the University of Miami. Together with fellow poet Carolyn Kizer, she first served on and then resigned from the Board of Chancellors of the Academy of American Poets.